DEPRESSION

Battling The Storm Within & Rising From Despair: A Personal And Practical Guide Through Depression

DEAN OTTO

Table of Contents

Introductory

Depression is a prevalent and critical mental health disorder distinguished by enduring emotions of melancholy, despair, and diminished engagement or enjoyment in routine responsibilities. It manifests as a disruption to an individual's daily functioning, surpassing the ordinary fluctuations that all individuals encounter.

Prominent symptoms of depression may encompass:

• Sad, apprehensive, or "empty" disposition: People diagnosed with depression frequently endure a pervasive sense of melancholy or emptiness that endures for the majority of the day, virtually on a daily basis.

• Decreased interest or delight in activities: An observable waning of interest or pleasure in formerly enjoyable pursuits, such as work, social interactions, or hobbies.

• Appetite or weight changes: Sufficient weight gain or loss, or alterations in appetite (e.g., excessive food or loss of appetite), are prevalent indications of depression.

• Sleep disturbances, including insomnia and oversleeping, may serve as indicators of depression. Certain people may experience challenges initiating slumber, whereas others may awaken excessively early and find it difficult to return to a state of rest.

• Loss of energy or general fatigue: A feeling of exhaustion and diminished vitality, persisting even during activities that do not require physical exertion.

• Emotions of remorse or worthlessness that are excessive in nature, frequently stemming from circumstances beyond the control of the individual.

• Difficulty concentrating, remembering details, or making decisions: Individuals diagnosed with depression may experience challenges with these cognitive functions.

• Psychiatric agitation or retardation is characterized by discernible alterations in bodily activity, including restlessness, delayed speech, and movements.

• Suicidal ideation or behavior: Severe manifestations of melancholy may manifest as suicidal thoughts or behaviors. It is imperative that anyone experiencing these thoughts seek professional assistance immediately.

Depression can arise from a confluence of biological, psychological, genetic, and environmental influences. A range of therapeutic modalities—psychotherapy, medication, and lifestyle modifications—can be efficacious in the management and amelioration of symptoms of this treatable condition.

Individuals exhibiting symptoms consistent with depression should promptly consult mental health professionals in order to receive an accurate diagnosis and appropriate treatment.

CHAPTER ONE

Varieties Of Depression

A variety of distinct forms of melancholy exist, each distinguished by its unique constellation of attributes and manifestations. The following are prevalent forms of depression:

• Major Depressive Disorder (MDD) is the most prevalent form of the depressive illness. Persistent sadness, hopelessness, and a loss of interest or enjoyment in daily activities are all characteristics of this condition. For symptoms to qualify as MDD, they must persist for a minimum of two weeks.

• Dysthymia, also known as Persistent Depressive Disorder, is a form of depression characterized by a minimum duration of two years (or one year for children and adolescents). Although the symptoms may not be as severe as those associated with major depression, they endure for an extended duration and have the potential to substantially disrupt daily activities.

• Bipolar Disorder, also known as Manic-Depressive Illness, is characterized by recurrent episodes of mania or hypomania interspersed with episodes of depression. A manic episode is characterized by heightened mood, increased energy, and impulsive behavior. Bipolar disorder is classified into various subtypes, Bipolar I and Bipolar II being among them.

• Seasonal Affective Disorder (SAD) is a form of melancholy that manifests during a particular period of the year, typically the autumn and winter seasons characterized by reduced sunlight exposure. Low energy, irritability, alterations in sleep patterns, and weight gain are all possible symptoms.

• Psychotic depression is characterized by the co-occurrence of profound depressive symptoms and psychotic manifestations, including hallucinations and delusions.

• Postpartum depression is a condition that certain women may encounter following childbirth. It is characterized by profound emotions of sorrow, anxiety, and fatigue. Changing hormone levels and the strain of neonatal care may both contribute to the development of this form of depression.

• Premenstrual Dysphoric Disorder (PMDD) is a severe manifestation of premenstrual syndrome (PMS) characterized by notable mood disruptions, including melancholy and irritability, that manifest during the last fortnight preceding menstruation.

• Atypical depression is distinguished by the presence of mood reactivity, wherein affected individuals undergo a mood elevation in reaction to positive stimuli. An increased appetite, weight gain, excessive sleep, and a cumbersome sensation in the limbs are additional possible symptoms.

• Situational depression, alternatively referred to as adjustment disorder with depressed mood, manifests in response to a particular life event or stressor. Instances of this disorder include bereavement, divorce, unemployment, or the loss of a loved one.

It is crucial to acknowledge that these classifications are not mutually exclusive; rather, an individual might exhibit a confluence of symptoms that correspond to distinct subtypes of depression. It is critical to obtain an accurate diagnosis from a mental health professional in order to formulate a suitable treatment strategy.

Depression's Neurobiology And Chemical Imbalances

Depression encompasses a multifaceted neurobiology that entails diverse alterations in the structure, function, and neurotransmitter activity of the brain. Despite the ongoing development of knowledge regarding the neurobiological mechanisms underlying melancholy, certain fundamental factors are frequently linked to the disorder:

1. Neurotransmitter Dysregulation:

• Serotonin is among the neurotransmitters that have been associated with depression. Serotonin is a mood regulator, and depressive symptoms are frequently correlated with reduced serotonin levels. A category of antidepressant drugs known as selective serotonin reuptake inhibitors (SSRIs) function by augmenting serotonin concentrations within the brain.

• Elevations in norepinephrine levels have also been associated with depressive symptoms. Norepinephrine influences mood, arousal, and attentiveness. Antidepressant medications that target norepinephrine reuptake include cyclic antidepressants and serotonin-norepinephrine reuptake inhibitors (SNRIs).

- Dopamine, an additional neurotransmitter, plays a role in the regulation of mood and the provision of rewards. Although the correlation between dopamine and depression is multifaceted, modifications in the functionality of dopamine have been identified in certain depressed individuals.

2. Reduced Hippocampal Volume:

- Research has indicated that depressed individuals may exhibit a reduced size of the hippocampus, a cerebral area that is implicated in memory and the regulation of emotions.

Frequently implicated in depression, chronic stress might be a contributing factor to this hippocampal volume reduction.

3. Prefrontal Cortex Impairment:

• Executive functions including problem-solving, decision-making, and emotional regulation are accomplished by the prefrontal cortex. Depressive disorders are characterized by alterations in the prefrontal cortex, such as diminished connectivity and activity.

4. Excessive amygdala activity:

• A region of the brain responsible for processing emotions, the amygdala, is frequently hyperactive in depressive patients. The increased level of activity could potentially be a factor in the development of negative emotional states and heightened sensitivity that are linked to the condition.

5. Neuroinflammation:

• An increasing body of evidence indicates a potential association between inflammation and depression. Chronic inflammation, which can arise from various sources including infections, stress, or other elements, has the potential to trigger or worsen depressive symptoms.

6. Contributing Genetic Factors:

• Genetic factors contribute to the predisposition of an individual to develop melancholy. Environmental stressors may elevate the risk of developing melancholy in individuals with specific genetic variations.

Individual differences and the complex neurobiology of depression are fundamental concepts that must be recognized. The "chemical imbalance" theory posits that depression is exclusively attributable to neurotransmitter imbalances; however, this oversimplification fails to encompass the entirety of the situation.

It is probable that depression arises from a confluence of genetic, environmental, and psychological influences.

Depression is frequently treated with a combination of pharmacotherapy, psychotherapy, and modifications to one's lifestyle. Antidepressant medications, including tricyclic antidepressants, SSRIs, and SNRIs, are designed to relieve depressive symptoms by modulating neurotransmitter activity.

CHAPTER TWO

The Value Of Open Communication

In numerous facets of human interaction, relationships, and problem-solving, open dialogue is vital. There are several critical domains in which open dialogue assumes an enormous role:

1. The Art of Communication:

• Dialogue without restrictions is essential for effective communication. It involves the open and honest expression of one's thoughts, emotions, and ideas. Open communication increases the likelihood that individuals will gain mutual understanding, resolve conflicts, and forge more robust relationships.

2. In terms of relationships:

• Open dialogue in interpersonal relationships cultivates comprehension, confidence, and closeness. The capacity to candidly communicate emotions and concerns fosters a sense of being listened to and assisted, thereby promoting the development of more robust and gratifying interpersonal connections.

3. Approaches to Problem Solving:

• Opening up for dialogue is crucial in the process of resolving problems and conflicts. Individuals and groups can identify common objectives, discuss differences, and collaborate to find solutions when they engage in candid and open dialogue.

4. The concept of teamwork:

• Open communication is vital for productive collaboration in a professional setting. The environment fosters the interchange of thoughts, evaluations, and beneficial critique. Open communication fosters greater innovation, adaptability, and productivity among members of a team.

5. One's Personal Development:

• It is essential for personal development to regularly engage in introspective and self-reflective dialogue with oneself. It facilitates the examination of one's thoughts, values, and aspirations, thereby fostering a more comprehensive comprehension of one's own being and objectives.

6. Cultivating Trust:

• Engaging in open dialogue is fundamental to establishing trust. An atmosphere of trust can be fostered when individuals engage in open and transparent communication. This holds true in workplaces, personal relationships, and societal interactions.

7. Psychological Health:

• The significance of open dialogue is heightened when discussing mental health. Promoting candid dialogues regarding mental health diminishes social stigma, empowers people to pursue assistance, and cultivates a more empathetic and tolerant community.

8. Cultural Comprehension:

• Open dialogue is crucial for promoting cultural understanding and tolerance in a globally diverse society. It enables individuals from various origins to exchange viewpoints, gain knowledge from one another, and construct connections that foster comprehension.

9. Resolving Conflicts:

• Isolation of opinion is an essential element of conflict resolution. By means of transparent communication, disputing parties are able to air their complaints, consider one another's viewpoints, and strive to identify areas of agreement or compromise.

10. Pioneering: Innovation

• Open dialogue fosters innovation through its promotion of unrestricted idea exchange. Individuals are more inclined to express their innovative ideas in environments that foster creativity and collaboration, where they perceive that their contributions are esteemed and acknowledged.

In general, open dialogue fosters an environment that encourages candor, compassion, and a collective recognition of human nature. Positive and supportive environments are critical for their establishment in various settings, including personal relationships, workplaces, communities, and broader societal contexts.

Seeking Assistance

Seeking assistance is an essential and brave course of action in confronting obstacles, be they of a personal nature, pertain to one's mental well-being, or encompass daily life complexities. If you're contemplating pursuing assistance, consider the following steps:

1. Recognize Your Emotions:

• Acknowledge and recognize your emotions and the difficulties you are experiencing. Diverse emotions are acceptable, and obtaining assistance is a proactive and positive decision.

2. Consult a Person You Can Trust:

• Opinion: Seek support from a trusted friend, family member, or individual. Engaging in a private conversation with a close acquaintance can offer valuable emotional solace and comprehension.

3. Contact a Professional in Mental Health:

• One may wish to consult with a mental health professional, including but not limited to a psychiatrist, psychologist, counselor, or therapist. These experts are credentialed to offer assistance and direction regarding a wide range of mental health issues.

4. Resources for Research:

• Determine which community or online resources are available for mental health. A plethora of organizations and helplines exist to furnish individuals grappling with mental health challenges with information, resources, and support.

5. Utilize Hotlines and Helplines:

• Helplines and hotlines are available to provide immediate assistance. There are helplines dedicated to mental health and crisis intervention in numerous nations. Frequently, these services are private and accessible around the clock.

6. Consult a Primary Care Physician by Visiting:

You should consider making an appointment with your primary care physician if you are uncertain about where to begin. They possess the ability to evaluate your circumstances, offer direction, and make appropriate mental health professional referrals.

7 .Gain Knowledge for Yourself:

• Increase your knowledge regarding the particular obstacles that you are encountering. Gaining an awareness of one's condition or circumstance can enhance one's sense of agency and facilitate more efficient communication with experts.

8 .Establish Practical Expectations:

- Although seeking assistance is a process, reasonable expectations must be established. Finding the appropriate treatment approach or professional may require some time, and progress may be gradual.

Bear in mind that asking for assistance is an indication of overcoming obstacles; you do not have to do so alone. People and resources are at your disposal to assist you on your path to wellness and recovery, whether you are navigating life transitions, mental health concerns, or relationship difficulties. I urge individuals who are in a critical situation or are grappling with suicidal or self-harming ideation to promptly contact emergency services or a crisis hotline.

CHAPTER THREE

Cognitive Behavioral Therapy

Cognitive Behavioral Therapy (CBT) is an extensively employed and empirically supported therapeutic modality that centers on the interrelation among thoughts, emotions, and actions.

Goal-oriented brief psychotherapy is a therapeutic approach that is intended to assist individuals in recognizing and altering maladaptive thought patterns and behaviors that are at the root of their challenges. Cognitive Behavioral Therapy (CBT) is frequently employed to treat anxiety disorders, depression, phobias, and various other mental health concerns due to its efficacy.

Fundamental CBT principles and techniques include:

1. The Restructuring of the Mind:

• CBT entails the process of recognizing and questioning maladaptive thought patterns and beliefs.

Cognitive restructuring or cognitive reframing is a cognitive process that assists individuals in substituting irrational or distorted thoughts with those that are more realistic and balanced.

2. Behavior Activation (BDA):

• Behavioral activation, an element of cognitive-behavioral therapy (CBT), centers on motivating individuals to participate in tasks that elicit feelings of enjoyment or achievement. This mitigates the avoidance and seclusion that are frequently symptoms of depression.

3. The use of exposure therapy:

• Prevalent applications of exposure therapy include the management of anxiety disorders, phobias, and post-traumatic stress disorder (PTSD). It assists individuals in overcoming anxiety or fear by exposing them to feared or avoided situations in a safe and gradual manner.

4. Approaches to Problem Solving:

• Individuals are taught effective problem-solving skills through CBT. Through the process of deconstructing complex issues into feasible components and formulating pragmatic resolutions, people can gain a sense of agency and diminish sentiments of powerlessness.

5. The following are mindfulness techniques:

• CBT frequently incorporates mindfulness, which is founded on the tenets of mindfulness-based cognitive therapy (MBCT) and mindfulness-based stress reduction (MBSR). Mindfulness techniques facilitate the cultivation of a more balanced perspective, the impartial observation of one's thoughts, and the maintenance of present-moment awareness.

6. Homework responsibilities:

• Between sessions, coursework is frequently assigned as part of CBT. The tasks may comprise monitoring one's thoughts and actions, honing recently acquired coping mechanisms, or participating in designated exercises to strengthen therapeutic objectives.

7. Target Setting:

• CBT is a goal-oriented approach in which clients and therapists collaborate to establish objectives that are both specific and attainable. The therapeutic process is guided by these objectives, which also serve as a framework for assessing progress.

8. A Therapeutic Partnership:

• In CBT, the therapeutic alliance is vital. The therapist and client engage in a supportive and cooperative partnership. While the therapist offers direction, feedback, and resources, the client participates actively in the therapeutic procedure.

Cognitive Behavioral Therapy (CBT) is commonly characterized by its structured nature, temporal restriction, and emphasis on the present moment, as opposed to an in-depth examination of past experiences.

It has the capacity to accommodate diverse cultural backgrounds and can be conducted either individually or in groups. CBT has been shown to be efficacious in ameliorating symptoms and enhancing functioning across a broad spectrum of mental health disorders.

Nevertheless, individual responses to therapy may differ in their efficacy;

therefore, it is critical to locate a therapist and approach that meet your specific requirements.

Meditation And Mindful Practice

Engaging in mindfulness and meditation entails the development of heightened consciousness, focused attention, and an impartial demeanor in the current moment.

Although frequently applied interchangeably, mindfulness is a more comprehensive notion that denotes a state of complete presence, whereas meditation pertains to particular practices or routines that foster mindfulness.

Although these practices originate from ancient contemplative traditions, their potential mental and physical health benefits have propelled them to pervasive popularity.

Practicing mindfulness:

1. Defined as:

The condition of attending to the present moment with receptiveness, inquisitiveness, and acceptance is known as mindfulness. The practice entails impartially observing one's thoughts and emotions, refraining from developing any emotional attachment or succumbing to them.

2. Strict Principles:

• Non-judgment entails the act of observing experiences without assigning either positive or negative evaluations to them.

• Non-striving: Being in the present moment without having any particular objective in mind.

• Beginner's Mind: Entering each moment with an empty and receptive mindset, devoid of any preconceived notions.

3. Requests for Applications:

• Mindfulness finds application in a multitude of contexts, encompassing mindful nutrition, mindfulness-based stress reduction (MBSR), and mindfulness-based cognitive therapy (MBCT). It is utilized to alleviate mental health issues, manage chronic pain, and reduce stress in clinical contexts.

Engaging in meditation:

1. Defined as:

Meditation is an umbrella term for a variety of practices designed to condition the mind to attain a state of increased awareness, concentration, and tranquility. A prevalent variety of meditation, mindfulness places great emphasis on the development of present-moment awareness.

2. Methods of Technique:

• Mindfulness meditation involves the deliberate concentration on bodily sensations, the breath, or an anchor in order to foster awareness.

• Loving-kindness Meditation: cultivating emotions of self-compassion and affection towards other individuals.

• Transcendental Meditation: attaining a state of tranquil alertness through the repetition of a mantra.

3. The benefits are:

• Meditation has been linked to a multitude of advantageous outcomes, encompassing the alleviation of tension, the enhancement of concentration and emotional well-being, and alterations in cerebral structure indicative of heightened gray matter density.

Methods for Engaging in Mindfulness Meditation:

1. Locate a Quiet Area:

• Select a comfortable, peaceful area where you will not be interrupted.

2. Maintain a relaxed posture:

• Assumes a comfortable seated or lying position. For support, you may utilize a chair or cushion.

3. Observe the Breath:

• Please focus your attention on inhaling and exhaling. Observe the inhalation and exhalation sensations.

4. Non-judgmental consciousness:

• To be without judgment as one permits thoughts and sensations to emerge. When the mind wanders, return attention to the respiration in a gentle manner.

5. Commence with Brief Sessions:

• It is advisable to commence with brief sessions, ranging from 5 to 10 minutes, and progressively extend the duration as one gains confidence.

6. Consistency Is Crucial:

• Consistent practice is imperative in order to fully benefit from the endeavor. The value of consistency surpasses that of time.

Mindfulness and meditation are both habitually incorporated practices that are accessible to individuals from diverse backgrounds. Beyond the reduction of tension, these practices also facilitate the enhancement of cognitive functions, the cultivation of a more profound self-awareness, and the exploration of personal experiences.

CHAPTER FOUR

Alterations To One's Lifestyle To Manage Depression

Modifications to one's lifestyle can have a substantial impact on the management and accommodation of melancholy.

Although not a replacement for therapeutic interventions, the integration of positive lifestyle practices can enhance overall well-being and serve as a valuable complement to professional treatment. Several modifications to one's lifestyle may be beneficial in assisting with depression.

1. Consistent Exercise:

• It has been demonstrated that regular physical activity exerts antidepressant properties. Physical activity induces the secretion of endorphins, brain compounds that function as endogenous mood enhancers. Yoga, walking, cycling, swimming, and similar activities can all be beneficial.

2. Diet:

• The relationship between nutrition and mental health is vital. A well-rounded dietary regimen comprising complex carbohydrates, lean proteins, fruits, vegetables, and whole foods can furnish vital nutrients that bolster cognitive processes. Additionally, fish, flaxseeds, and walnuts contain omega-3 fatty acids, which may have mood-boosting properties.

3. Sufficient Sleep:

• Developing and maintaining regular sleep schedules is critical for one's mental health. Aim for seven to nine hours of restful sleep per night. Establish a calming twilight routine, refrain from consuming stimulants prior to sleep, and adhere to a regular sleep schedule.

4. Techniques for Relaxation and Mindfulness:

• Progressive muscle relaxation, mindfulness meditation, and deep breathing exercises are all beneficial practices that can aid in stress management and foster a state of tranquility. By incorporating these techniques into one's daily regimen, one can alleviate anxiety and enhance mood.

5. Social Relationship:

• Maintain relationships with family and acquaintances. Support from others is vital for one's emotional health. To combat feelings of isolation, confide in dependable individuals, engage in social activities, and attend group events.

6. Restrict Use of Alcohol and Substances:

• Alcohol and substance abuse in excess can exacerbate the symptoms of depression. As they may impede treatment and worsen mood fluctuations, alcohol and illicit substances should be consumed in moderation or completely abstained from.

7. Develop a Routine:

• To establish a consistent daily regimen, incorporate regular mealtimes, physical activity, and adequate rest. Managing depressive symptoms may be facilitated by the stability and predictability that a structured routine can provide.

8. Set Realistic Objectives:

• Deconstruct assignments into more manageable objectives. Acknowledge accomplishments, irrespective of their magnitude, and refrain from establishing impracticable anticipations. Developing and achieving attainable objectives has the potential to enhance one's self-esteem.

9. Reduce Stressors:

• Determine the origins of tension in your life and investigate strategies to mitigate or control them. This may entail establishing limits, assigning responsibilities, or acquiring stress-reduction strategies.

10. The Restructuring of the Mind:

• One should confront detrimental thought patterns and substitute them with more rational and balanced viewpoints. Techniques of cognitive-behavioral therapy (CBT) may be useful for altering negative thought patterns.

11. Participate in Pleasurable Activities:

• Engage in activities that elicit feelings of happiness and achievement. Participating in enjoyable activities, such as engaging in creative pursuits, spending time in nature, or pursing personal hobbies, has the potential to have a positive influence on one's mood.

It is essential to observe that changes in lifestyle may not be adequate on their own to treat severe depression. In certain instances, professional assistance, including psychotherapy and medication, may be required. It is imperative that you or a loved one who is exhibiting indications of depression seek the assistance of a mental health practitioner in order to receive a thorough evaluation and individualized treatment strategy.

Constructing A Support Network

Establishing a robust support network is vital for one's emotional welfare and can prove particularly advantageous when contending with difficulties like melancholy.

A support system comprises members who offer one another emotional, practical, and occasionally monetary assistance in times of adversity. Implement the following measures to construct and fortify your support network:

1. Determining Supportive People:

• Determine which individuals in your life are compassionate, understanding, and encouraging. This may consist of mentors, family members, acquaintances, and coworkers. Seek companions who possess an uplifting impact and sincerely concern themselves with your welfare.

2. Communicate in an Open Fashion:

• I encourage you to be candid and forthright regarding your emotions and personal encounters. Dissidentize your thoughts and inform your support network of the challenges you are currently facing. Sincerity in communication is critical for establishing confidence and comprehension.

3. Promote Knowledge Among Your Support System:

• Assist those close to you in comprehending melancholy, including its nature, impact, and potential avenues for support. Providing accurate information about mental health can dispel falsehoods and misunderstandings.

4. Establish Practical Expectations:

• Effectively convey your requirements and anticipations. Inform your support network of your needs and preferences regarding the type of assistance that would be most beneficial. Be pragmatic regarding the capabilities they can impart.

5. Consolidate Your Support System:

• It is advantageous to possess a varied support network comprising a variety of relationship categories. Although close family and friends are indispensable, community groups, support organizations, and therapy may also provide assistance.

6. Join Groups of Support:

• It is advisable to contemplate participating in a support group that caters to individuals encountering comparable obstacles. This can foster a sense of community, facilitate the exchange of coping strategies, and promote mutual understanding.

7. Professional Assistance:

• One should consider seeking professional support from mental health professionals, in addition to intimate connections. Support hotlines, therapists, or counselors are all viable resources that can offer specialized guidance and assistance.

8. Be an Encouraged Friend:

• Establishing a support system is a two-way street. It is probable that your peers and loved ones will reciprocate your support if you are present for them in times of need. Support for one another fortifies relationships.

9. Attend Social Occasions:

• Engage in social events and activities in order to broaden your social circle. This may afford you the chance to encounter new individuals who have the potential to form your support network.

10. Engage in active listening by:

• Exhibit active listening during the expression of others' thoughts and emotions. Excellent listening skills cultivate more robust interpersonal bonds and serve as an indication of a readiness to assist others.

11. Maintain Connections Online:

• In the contemporary digital era, maintaining connections does not invariably necessitate in-person engagement. Leverage technological advancements to maintain communication with family and friends, particularly those who are located in different geographic locations.

12. Seek Expert Assistance:

• In cases of severe depression, it is imperative to obtain professional assistance. Guidance and targeted support can be obtained from mental health professionals, including therapists and counselors.

Keep in mind that establishing a support system requires time, and that starting modest is acceptable. Develop relationships that make a positive contribution to your overall well-being, and do not hesitate to seek assistance when necessary.

The process of constructing a support system is continuous, and the relationships one forges can prove to

be of immense value when
confronting the difficulties that arise
throughout one's existence.

CHAPTER FIVE

Navigating Relapses And Conquering Obstacles

Overcoming obstacles and coping with relapses are crucial components of the recovery process, particularly when melancholy is involved. The following tactics should assist you in navigating and surmounting obstacles:

1. Developing Self-Compassion:

• Self-compassion should guide your behavior. Recognize that setbacks are inevitable and that experiencing periods of difficulty is acceptable. To cultivate self-compassion and prevent self-blame, treat yourself with the same benevolence that you would extend to a friend in a comparable circumstance.

2. Determine Patterns and Triggers:

• Consider the various elements that might have played a role in the setback. Determine the potential triggers, stressors, or patterns that influenced the event. Gaining knowledge of these factors can assist in the formulation of future strategies for their more efficient management.

3. Seek Out Assistance:

• One should discuss their experience with a mental health professional, trusted family members, or acquaintances. Engaging in dialogue regarding setbacks can yield emotional solace, present alternative viewpoints, and mitigate feelings of isolation.

4. Analyze Coping Methods:

• Reevaluate and reassess the coping mechanisms that have demonstrated efficacy in previous instances. Determine which methods have proven to be efficacious and contemplate integrating them into your regimen with greater regularity.

5. Modify Anticipations:

• Modify your expectations and establish attainable objectives. Acknowledge that advancements may encounter obstacles, and that progress is frequently an incremental one. Deconstruct more ambitious objectives into more manageable and incremental advances.

6. Reevaluate and adjust therapeutic regimens:

• Reevaluate and consult with a mental health professional regarding your treatment plan. On the basis of your present requirements, it might be necessary to modify therapeutic approaches, medications, or other interventions.

7. Prioritize Self-Care:

• To enhance one's overall health and well-being, make self-care activities that are enjoyable and involve regular exercise, nutritious eating, and sufficient sleep a top priority. It is imperative to prioritize one's physical and emotional well-being when confronted with difficult circumstances.

8. Gain Knowledge from Setbacks:

• Consider setbacks as learning and development opportunities. Reflect on the knowledge that can be gleaned from the experience and devise strategies to implement these insights in order to manage forthcoming challenges more effectively.

9. Consciousness and Release:

• Develop an awareness of and acceptance of the present moment. One should redirect their attention from past setbacks and future concerns towards the present moment, demonstrating a non-judgmental acceptance of their current circumstances.

10. Develop an Emergency Plan:

• Construct a crisis plan in conjunction with the assistance of a mental health professional. A comprehensive plan may encompass precise actions, contacts, and coping mechanisms that are to be executed in the face of adversity.

11. Commemorate Minor Accomplishments:

• Celebrate and acknowledge modest accomplishments, even if they appear insignificant. Even the smallest amount of progress acknowledged can increase one's confidence and motivation.

12. Examine Novel Methodologies:

• Be receptive to investigating novel methodologies or interventions. If past approaches have failed to produce the intended outcomes, contemplate experimenting with alternative methodologies or pursuing supplementary assistance.

It is crucial to retain in mind that encountering obstacles is an inherent aspect of the process of recuperation, and to confront them with fortitude and perseverance. It is imperative to seek professional guidance if you encounter persistent or overpowering setbacks, as this will enable you to develop a customized approach that effectively addresses your unique requirements.

Discovery Of Oneself And Healing

The processes of self-discovery and healing are intricately linked, as they both entail the acquisition of self-awareness, the comprehension of previous encounters, and the pursuit of individual development and wellness. Key principles and strategies for self-discovery and healing include the following:

The process of self-discovery

1. Consider One's Beliefs and Values:

• Set aside some time to consider your fundamental values and beliefs. What is most important to you? Recognizing and appreciating one's personal values can provide direction for one's choices and behaviors.

2. Examine One's Passions and Interests:

• Identify personal activities and interests that elicit feelings of pleasure and satisfaction. Participating in pursuits that ignite one's passion can significantly enhance one's sense of purpose.

3. Consideratory Self-Reflection:

• Consistent self-reflection entails the process of scrutinizing one's own thoughts, emotions, and actions. The practice of mindfulness or journaling may aid in this endeavor.

4. Evaluation of Strengths and Weaknesses:

• Identify your areas of improvement and areas of strength. Recognizing and accepting one's assets and weaknesses can enhance the development of a more harmonious self-image.

5. Appreciate Curiosity:

• Make an effort to be receptive to novel concepts, experiences, and viewpoints. Curiosity cultivates awe and an ongoing pursuit of knowledge regarding one's own being and the surrounding environment.

6. Require Feedback:

• It is advisable to seek feedback from reliable individuals such as trusted acquaintances, family, or mentors. Unsuspecting insights from others may prove to be equally valuable.

7. Confront Restrictive Beliefs:

• One should recognize and confront constraining beliefs that could be impeding progress. In lieu of negative self-talk, adopt more affirming and positive beliefs.

The healing process:

1.   Recognize   and   Validate Emotions:

• Permit yourself to recognize and validate your emotions, notwithstanding their inherent difficulty. It is instrumental in the healing process that you acknowledge and accept your emotions.

2. Engage in Self-Compassion:

• I particularly encourage you to practice self-compassion and kindness during difficult circumstances. Being compassionate and understanding with oneself constitutes self-compassion.

3. Establish Boundaries:

• Maintaining and establishing healthy boundaries in activities and relationships is essential. Establishing boundaries promotes autonomy and safeguards one's well-being.

4. To be forgiven:

• To begin with, contemplate the application of forgiveness to oneself and others. Forgiveness is not synonymous with condoning wrongdoing; rather, it signifies the release of the emotional weight that accompanies resentment.

5. Therapeutic Assistance:

• If necessary, pursue therapy or counseling. A mental health professional possesses the ability to offer direction, assistance, and resources to assist individuals in managing previous traumatic incidents or difficult life circumstances.

6. Zen-practice and meditation:

• By practicing mindfulness and meditation, one can cultivate a sense of inner peace and remain in the present moment. By observing one's thoughts and emotions with mindfulness, one can avoid becoming overcome by them.

7. Creatively express yourself by:

• Investigate artistic, literary, or musical pursuits as means of expressing one's emotions and personal experiences. Creative expression has the potential to serve as a potent means of catharsis.

8. Establish Relationships with Supportive Communities:

• Participate in online communities or support groups to establish connections with individuals who have encountered comparable challenges. Support and mutual understanding can play a crucial role in facilitating the healing process.

9. Commemorate Advances:

• Commemorate minor triumphs and significant junctures along your path to recovery. Acknowledge the advancements that have been achieved, regardless of their incremental nature.

10. Developing Gratitude:

• Developing an attitude of gratitude involves directing one's attention towards the favorable facets of one's life. Frequent expressions of gratitude can alter one's outlook and foster a state of overall wellness.

Constant efforts at healing and self-discovery require self-awareness, self-compassion, and a dedication to individual development. It is critical to approach these endeavors with fortitude, perseverance, and an openness to change. Seeking expert assistance or recourse can be beneficial if one encounters difficulty or feels overwhelmed throughout the process.

CHAPTER SIX

Preserving Psychological Well-Being And Promoting Resilience

Ensuring mental health and cultivating resilience are fundamental components of holistic wellness, particularly when confronted with the difficulties and pressures of daily life. The following are some methods for fostering mental health and resiliency:

Habits of Daily Living for Mental Health:

1. Implement a Routine:

• Establish a consistent sleep schedule, eat at regular intervals, and set aside time each day for work, relaxation, and self-care. Stability may be enhanced by the presence of predictability.

2. Physical Activity:

• Irregularly participate in physical exercise. It has been demonstrated that physical activity improves mood and mental health. Participate in enjoyable activities such as dancing, yoga, walking, or jogging.

3. Optimal Nutrition:

• Maintain a nutritious and well-balanced diet. Foods abundant in nutrients promote physical and mental health as a whole. Reduce the quantity of processed and sugary snacks consumed.

4. Sufficient Sleep:

• It is essential to give precedence to getting enough quality sleep. Aim for 7-9 hours of sleep per night, establish a bedtime routine, and create a comfortable sleeping environment.

5. Zen-practice and meditation:

• Engage in mindfulness and meditation as a means to reduce stress and remain in the present moment. One can cultivate a sense of calm and manage anxious thoughts through the use of these techniques.

6. Maintain Contact:

• Cultivate connections with family, friends, and the community. Social connections foster a sense of belonging and provide assistance.

7. Regulate Display Time:

• Limit your time spent in front of screens, particularly social media. Overindulgence in digital devices may have adverse effects on mental health and stress levels.

8. Interests and Creative Pursuits:

• Participate in enjoyable activities that foster a sense of achievement. Hobbies and creative pursuits offer individuals a constructive means of self-expression and relaxation.

9. Acquire the Ability to Say No:

• Learn to establish limits and say no when appropriate. Overcommitment can result in burnout and stress.

10. Engage in Gratitude:

• Develop an attitude of gratitude by recognizing and valuing the positive aspects of your life on a consistent basis. Practicing gratitude can help you concentrate on the positive.

Constructing Resilience:

1. A Positive Attitude:

• One can foster a positive mindset by shifting attention from problems to potential solutions. Develop a positive outlook and engage in the process of reframing negative thoughts.

2. The quality of adaptability

• One should embrace change and cultivate adaptability. Individuals who are resilient are adaptable and capable of adjusting to new situations.

3. Skills for Solving Problems:

• Improve one's problem-solving abilities in order to adeptly navigate obstacles. Deconstruct problems into feasible components and ascertain operational resolutions.

4. Request Support:

• Construct a robust support network. Seek assistance from family, friends, or a therapist if you require emotional support. By divulging your difficulties, you may alleviate some of the strain.

5. Developing Self-Compassion:

• Practice self-compassion and kindness. It is advisable to extend the same compassion and regard for oneself as one would to a friend who is encountering challenges.

6. MBSR: Mindfulness-Based Stress Reduction:

• One should contemplate engaging in mindfulness-based programs such as MBSR. These programs promote resilience and instruct stress reduction techniques.

7. Gain Knowledge from Setbacks:

• Consider setbacks as learning and development opportunities. Determining insights from obstacles and implementing them in subsequent circumstances.

8. Sustain a Clarity of Objective:

• One should ascertain their personal values and sustain a sense of direction. Your actions and decisions may be influenced by your deepest values.

9. Develop Effective Coping Mechanisms:

• One can cultivate effective coping strategies to manage stress, including but not limited to progressive muscle relaxation, deep breathing, and participation in pleasurable activities.

10. Professional Assistance:

• When necessary, consult with a professional for assistance. Counselors and therapists are capable of offering direction and techniques for developing resilience.

Bear in mind that mental health is a personalized and ever-changing journey. Should you encounter difficulties in executing these strategies or if these obstacles continue to persist, you may wish to contemplate seeking professional advice.

Mental health professionals are capable of offering individualized assistance and aiding in the formulation of a customized strategy that meets your specific requirements.

Summary

Placing mental health as a top priority and cultivating resilience are fundamental elements of a gratifying and well-rounded existence. The interconnectedness of the aforementioned strategies for fostering resilience and maintaining mental health underscores the significance of adopting a comprehensive approach to overall well-being. Listed below are several important takeaways:

1. Whole-Self Wellness:

• Mental health is intricately connected to a multitude of facets of existence, encompassing personal fulfillment, relationships, and daily routines. An all-encompassing approach takes into account the interdependence of these elements.

• The Importance of Daily Practices: The establishment and maintenance of healthy daily practices make a substantial contribution to one's mental health. A bedrock for wellness is comprised of regular activities, nourishing sustenance, exercise, and restful slumber.

• The Relationship Between Mindfulness and Resilience: o Mindfulness exercises, including meditation and cultivating a state of present-moment awareness, have the potential to bolster mental fortitude. These behaviors foster an optimistic perspective, mitigate anxiety, and aid in the maintenance of emotional equilibrium.

• Social Relationship: Establishing and sustaining significant social connections serves as a potent safeguard against mental health issues. Solid interpersonal connections foster encouragement, comprehension, and a feeling of inclusion.

• Growth and Adaptability: o Resilience is characterized by the capacity to learn and develop in the face of adversity. Resilience is enhanced by adopting a proactive attitude, considering alternative solutions, and embracing change.

• The cultivation of self-compassion is fundamental to the process of attaining and maintaining optimal mental health. Promoting self-care, being considerate of one's own shortcomings and strengths, and being kind to oneself all contribute to the development of a positive self-image. The process of self-discovery entails the investigation of one's own values, interests, and development.

• Seeking professional assistance is considered a demonstration of fortitude. Mental health professionals are capable of offering individualized guidance, therapeutic interventions, and tools.

• Commemorate Progress: It is imperative to recognize and commemorate minor triumphs and significant achievements. Acknowledging even small steps of progress serves to strengthen one's sense of achievement and motivation.

• Resilience in the Face of Adversity: o Although setbacks are an inevitable aspect of existence, our response to them reveals our resilience. By perceiving setbacks as occasions for growth, learning, and adaptation, one can enhance their long-term well-being.

• Continuous Process: Mental health and resilience are continuous processes that demand dedication, introspection, and a commitment to individual development. It is crucial to exercise self-control and consistently evaluate and adapt strategies in response to changing circumstances.

Bear in mind that each individual's trajectory is distinct, and a universal strategy for mental health and resilience does not exist. Constructing a gratifying and harmonious existence necessitates cognizance of and regard for personal requirements, solicitation of assistance when required, and acceptance of the ever-changing nature of one's well-being.

THE END